faith

D1711933

faith

STORIES OF BELIEF AND SPIRITUALITY

Edited by Jon Barrett and Megan Howard

AVON BOOKS
An Imprint of HarperCollins Publishers

Photo Credits

Permission to use the following photographs is gratefully acknowledged: page x, © Julie Blattberg; page 6, © Meghan Hoover; page 20, © Art Streiber; page 28, Britt J. Erlanson-Messens/Imagebank; page 40, © Chris Anderson/ Aurora; page 44, © Kathleen Flanigan; page 48, © Michael Carroll; page 50, © Eric O'Connell; page 56, © Donna Day; page 60, © David Gould/Imagebank; page 68, © Mando Gonzales; page 78, courtesy of Willa Ford; page 84, © William R. Sallaz; page 90, © Jeaneen Lund; page 100, Nicolas Russell/Imagebank; page 108, courtesy of Amanda Groaning; page 116, courtesy of Jeanine Jackson; page 122, © Gregory Pace/Corbis SYGMA.

Faith: Stories of Belief and Spirituality

The following chapters were originally published in *Teen People* magazine:
"John Rzeznik: This Doll's Life" (April 1999)
"Choosing My Religion" (January 1999)
"Julie Stoffer: Keeping the Faith" (February 2001)
"Craig Scott: Remembering Rachel" (August 1999)

Library of Congress Catalog Card Number: 2001117189
ISBN 0-06-447321-X

First Avon edition, 2001

AVON TRADEMARK REG. U.S. PAT. OFF. AND IN OTHER COUNTRIES,
MARCA REGISTRADA, HECHO EN U.S.A.

Visit us on the World Wide Web!
www.harperteen.com
www.teenpeople.com
AOL Keyword: Teen People

To all the teens who have shared
their stories with us.

Contents

Letter from the Editor

In our tell-all culture, where people expose their inner demons on TV and in chat rooms every day, it's remarkable that we often shy away from discussions of faith. Religion—like sex and politics—is a conversational quagmire, we're told. Surely, it is a personal topic, but talking about spirituality can also enrich our lives immensely, as we can see in the essays here, in which writers fearlessly wrestle with these emotions and address some of life's most complex questions: How do you maintain faith in the face of tragedy? How do you find inner peace in a chaotic world? What happens when your beliefs differ from those of your friends and family?

Questions of tradition loom large in the lives of teens like Hakim Muhammad, a Muslim, and Abby Calm, an Orthodox Jew. Both chose to live by the strict laws their religions dictate, even though they have openly questioned some of these traditions. On the opposite side of the spectrum, teens like Marlires Fitch, a Methodist, and Leah Sell, a Wiccan, chose to distance themselves from the religions they were born into and instead they hand-picked ones that better suited their beliefs. Julie Stoffer, a

Mormon, had her religious convictions tested when she participated in MTV's *The Real World*. Though her religion forbids premarital sex, drinking, smoking and homosexuality, Julie was exposed to these things every day and had to determine what she believed as opposed to what her religion taught her to believe. Some of our writers found salvation and solace outside of organized religion. When John Rzeznik of the Goo Goo Dolls lost both of his parents at age seventeen, he poured his heart into music, while Jennifer Howitt, a paraplegic, found that playing basketball, even while confined to a wheelchair, was a saving grace.

As our writers attest, spirituality takes many forms. For some, this means belief in a higher power; for others, like Justin Jeffre of 98°, spirituality simply means taking a walk in the woods. Whatever their definitions of faith, their stories prove that spirituality is not only a topic worthy of exploration, but an essential part of who we are.

Barbara O'Dair
Managing Editor, *Teen People*

justin jeffre:
the search for
INNER PEACE

As a member of the hot band 98°, Justin Jeffre must constantly battle the pressures of success. Here, he reveals how his faith—in himself and in God—helps him deal with it all.

Justin Jeffre, as told to Jon Barrett

I'm not a theologian or anything, but faith has always played an important role in my life. Not just religious faith (I was brought up with what my parents were into, the Catholic Church), but also faith in myself— that I would be successful in my pursuit of a music career and be in a group like the one I'm actually in today.

Looking back, it's easy for me to see how these different aspects of faith have worked hand in hand throughout my life. For instance, I always knew growing up that if I both believed in God and worked hard, I would have no trouble fulfilling my dreams. It wasn't like I said to myself, "OK, I'm going to be a rock star and I believe in God, so I don't have to go to school." I worked really hard—both in school (I was a history major at the University of Cincinnati) and as a musician. But it was faith in God and in myself that gave me the motivation to get through the necessary grunt work to get where I wanted to be.

It also gave me—as well as the other guys in 98°, Nick and Drew Lachey and Jeff Timmons—the guts to take that important "leap of faith" when so many people said we wouldn't make it as a band. We weren't the first four guys from Ohio to drop everything to move to Los Angeles to pursue our dreams—and we won't be the last. But for some reason it worked for us. Thinking about it today, I can't believe ours was just a case of hard work and dumb luck. There must have been a higher power looking out for our best interest.

Religion, however, is a very personal thing. You can take a hundred Christians from the same denomination and the exact same church and you would get a hundred different opinions about what it is they're being taught. For me, even though I was raised Catholic and had a strong faith in God, going to church always felt like simply going through the motions.

It can be that way with anything you do again and again. Even when performing, which I *love* to do, I sometimes become immune to all the excited and screaming fans around me. Being on the road can become so repetitive that it takes something out of the norm to wake me up to the reality of "Wow, I can't believe I'm really standing here with these guys getting this reaction."

Closer to God

When it came to church, there just wasn't anything to wake me up and convince me that I should be there every Sunday. Don't get me wrong, I'm not bashing my Catholic upbringing. It's an important part of who I am today and it provided a strong foundation for what I believe today. It's just that as I've grown older, I've realized that I feel much closer to God when I'm in the woods or in some other natural surrounding, listening to the birds and experiencing the world the way it was meant to be experienced. Whether it's looking at the ocean, a lake, or a stream, that's where I now find peace—not in the rituals of organized religion.

Not that I don't think there are lessons to be learned from organized religion. In addition to my Catholic upbringing, I've studied Eastern religions, such as Taoism and Buddhism, as well as Native American traditions in an attempt to figure out religion's role in my life. What I've learned is that what's really important to me, when it comes to maintaining my faith in myself and in God, is finding a sense of inner peace.

Simple Abundances

That might sound easy at first. But it's more apparent to me every day that the world is a crazy, messed-up, stressful place. And when it comes to the music business, all the horror stories you've heard are true. There are a lot of sharks out there looking to take a bite out of you, and there are very few folks you can trust. It's also easy to get wrapped up in the hype that surrounds all popular musicians and, in turn, lose your focus on the people and things that mean the most to you.

Rather than go to church when things are all out of whack, I make a conscious effort to stop and find peace within myself. Although I like the outdoors, this doesn't take hours of wandering through the woods. I just need to find a quiet spot where I can sit down, stretch my body a little, focus on my breathing, and concentrate on clearing my cluttered mind.

If this still sounds simple, keep in mind that sometimes it's the simple things that are the most difficult to understand. I don't even know if I understand it all myself. I do know, however, that when I relax like this, I focus on the things that are important to me, I have a better understanding of the person I'm supposed to be, and, most importantly, I feel closer than ever to my faith in God and in myself.

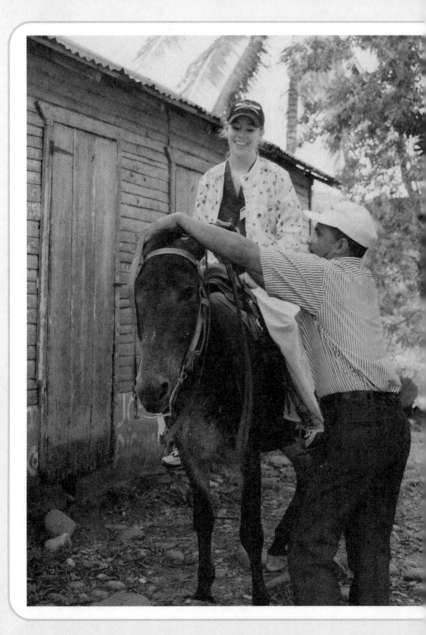

Chapter 2

meghan hoover: MISSIONARY GIRL

Meghan Hoover shares how a two-week mission trip in Latin America taught her much more than she ever expected.

Meghan Hoover

May 19, 2000

I am so excited! Lili, a close friend from home, is traveling with me to Ecuador. We are volunteering with MMI, Medical Ministry International, which is an organization that travels throughout the world and provides medical attention to the poor. MMI is a Christian group. While I'm going with them to help the people of Ecuador, for me, I believe the entire experience will strengthen my already close relation-ship to God. Lili and I will be working as translators for doctors and nurses.

6:30 A.M.

Lili and I are in the car right now on our way to Newark Airport. First stop, Miami, then it's on to Quito, Ecuador.

8:50 A.M.

Right now I'm in Quito. While we were in the airport, we met up with three other MMI workers—Ashley, Sharon and John. John is a physician, and Sharon, his wife, will be a general helper. Ashley is one of the teenagers, and Lili and I are rooming with her tonight. We are having such fun, it is hard to settle down to sleep.

I'm really anxious to get started. My Spanish is much better than when I went to the Dominican Republic on the last mission trip. Even though I feel more fluent than before, I am still very nervous. What if I say the wrong thing to the doctor? Or what if I can't understand what the patient is saying? I just hope that when I start tomorrow, every worry will disappear.

9:00 P.M.

We arrived too late in Otavalo to make it to the work site, so we were given permission by the project director, Mesa, to shop in the markets. It is a very large park filled with booths of sweaters, shoes, bags, table-cloths, hammocks and jewelry, and the list goes on and on. Later, we met all the other MMI participants. The other teenagers are not as goofy and outgoing as Ashley, Lili and I, but they are very cool.

I'm going to go to sleep now, with great room-mates and a very exciting two-week adventure just around the corner.

martes, el 20 de junio, 2000   / **Día 3** /

Today, I got up at 6:00 A.M. for breakfast. At the end of every breakfast we have a devotion that is led by one of the participants reading parts of the Bible. Then we left on buses for a village, Chota, which is about one hour away. Chota is an impoverished community of people whose ancestors came here as part of the European cotton and fruit slave trade.

We set up our clinic in the little four-room elementary school. The bathroom contained two stalls with inoperable doors and no running water. The dirt road leading from the highway to the school had been washed away by the raging river one week before we arrived. Most patients had bacterial and bronchial infections, worms and rashes.

Lili and I worked in the *charla*, which is the health education center, handing out and explaining prescriptions, teaching the importance of drinking enough water, brushing teeth and bathing. Throughout the day, children would stand at the windows and listen to the patient consultations, watch the pharmacy and beg for attention from whoever would give it to them. I noticed that most of the patients didn't mind that they were being watched.

miércoles, el 21 de junio, 2000   / **Día 4** /

Wow, what a day! Everyone went to either the Otavalo Hospital or to the Atuntaki Clinic. We set up a clinic in a small, one-room church. We used benches to create five different stations for the doctors and translators. It was not very private, but it didn't bother the patients.

Patients came in with problems that Americans think of as routine—headaches, backaches, runny noses and sore eyes. However, others came in needing surgery of some sort. The majority of them needed hernia or gall bladder operations. Many women had vaginal infections. Some patients came to us with serious problems that we could not fix with medicine; with others we were unprepared to perform the necessary surgery. It was difficult to tell them we couldn't help. But we would give them a referral to a hospital in Quito for a follow-up consultation.

I was surprised, however, that when I told the patients they needed an operation, they were not more upset or worried. Many were so thankful that they would start crying and repeatedly tell us that the doctor and I were angels. Then I was given the opportunity to observe an operation! I saw two hernias removed. One was from a little four-year-old boy. The other patient was an elderly man. I stayed with him throughout, finding a gown for him, taking him to the operating room and staying with him while the anesthesiologist prepared him for the operation. I talked to him to ease his worries until he fell asleep. I then watched as they cut him open, removed the hernia, and stitched him back up. It was unforgettable. Neither operation was nearly as bad as I had anticipated. Normally I cringe and turn away at the sight of blood, but today was great.

Later, I returned to translating, where I probably had the single most incredible conversation of my life. A woman sat down and began telling us about how she had lost two children, one at birth and another in an automobile accident. She desperately wanted another child but was afraid that she couldn't have one because she had cancer. When Dr. John examined her he found that she did not have cancer, so she could have another baby. When I told her, she began to weep tears of joy. Her happiness was so true and beautiful.

Shortly after this woman left, another woman entered with a three-year-old that could not talk, walk, run or engage in any other typical activity. His mother wondered what was wrong with him and if she had done something wrong. Dr. John told me to tell her that her child's brain was not fully developed. The only thing she could do for him was keep loving him. It was very difficult telling her this because I could see how much she loved her child. She kept asking, *"¿No hay algo pueden hacer?"* ("Isn't there anything we can do?") All I could say was, *"Su amor es la mejor cosa para el."* ("Your love is the best thing for him.") I hope I don't have to do anything like that again.

jueves, el 22 de junio, 2000   / **Día 5** /

Today was incredible. I translated again for Dr. John, and many different people came in needing various exams. One woman was in extreme pain. Dr.

John examined her and found out she had hemor-rhoids. While Dr. John was examining her, Lili and I stood on chairs and held up a small sheet so that the other patients waiting would not stare. I could see her trying so hard not to scream or yell; she was being so brave. I have difficulty seeing the patients in pain. Of course, I talk with the patients and try to make them feel better by holding their hands and reassuring them, but I can't do everything, and that's what hurts.

viernes, el 23 de junio, 2000   / **Día 6** /

Today I had to tell an absolutely sweet and beauti-ful seventy-year-old woman that she had cancer and would only live for about two more weeks. The cancer had started in her stomach and spread to her back, breasts and liver. When I told both this woman and her daughter, they just sat there, not one tear in either's eyes. Yesterday I told a woman she could bring children into our world, and today I had to tell another that she was about to die. This is quite a contrast.

sábado, el 24 de junio, 2000   / **Día 7** /

This afternoon while we were walking down the street, I heard a loud *bang* and then suddenly there was the *worst* stench. It burned and stung my eyes, mouth, throat and nose. The entire town walked around with clothing covering their noses and mouths—the entire town! We found out that people from the surrounding mountains had come for solstice festivities and some of them were known to get drunk and get in fights. In past years, because there had been some deaths, the police had decided to use tear gas to control the fighting. Before I found out what the problem was, I thought everyone was going to die. It was very scary.

Tonight in town there were Ecuadorian *fiestas*. Townspeople were dancing around the streets and in restaurants in Halloween-like costumes. We joined a few different groups as they danced up the streets and then were invited inside their homes. We were honored to be included in the festivities and welcomed into their houses. We didn't go back to the hotel until 12:00.

domingo, el 25 de junio, 2000   / **Día 8** /

I am so tired! After a church service, most MMI people took a hike to a very high waterfall. Some people decided to stop at the waterfall, but some of us continued to hike. When we arrived at the top of a cliff, we saw an old lady sitting in a cornfield with her sheep and dog. We talked with her and learned that she walks up here every day so her sheep can graze. She sits there for four hours, looking at the view. What a treasure to spend so much time in such harmony! In the United States, we study hard, work hard and play hard, without really taking time to appreciate the beauty in front of us. Around 6:15, we walked back. The hike was probably about six hours long, and although my legs are really hurting right now, it was definitely worth it.

lunes, el 26 de junio, 2000 / **Día 9** /

Today I almost passed out while watching a hernia surgery. The sight of blood really bothered me. I needed to lie down for a while but I was fine after I drank some water and relaxed.

After work I again walked around town with everyone. I feel so safe here in Otavalo. It has become a new home. I honestly have never met such a great bunch of people. Everyone is so different but amazing in a special way.

martes, el 27 de junio, 2000 / **Día 10** /

I was tired and sick this morning, so I slept until about 1:30 P.M. After I got up, I took a taxi to the hospital but, because I was late, I could not assist in any surgeries—medical rules. So the only thing I did all day was sit and watch the room that has all of our cameras, money, clothing and medicines. I really did not like doing this because I hate feeling useless. I understand there are many different jobs that need to be shared, but I just wished that I could be more helpful.

Today was probably the best day of the entire trip. First thing this morning I was able to observe a cesarean performed by the Ecuadorian doctors. I felt disgusted at the sight of blood yet delighted to be witnessing this miracle of birth. Right when I was about to leave I saw the baby girl's head and, at that moment, I started crying. I was witnessing the birth of one of God's children!

This mission has really showed me what I want in my life. I want to continue with mission work all over the world, especially in Latin American countries. Everything about this trip has made it perfect: the people, the missionary work, the Ecuadorians, making and meeting friends for life, and spreading, celebrating and teaching others about God.

I can't believe today was our last day! Today I assisted in a surgery—a hernia operation. I loved it! And I didn't even get light-headed or have to sit down or anything. I was standing up for the entire hour, holding back skin, getting bloody, but healing a man. I am thinking about going into medicine, maybe pediatrics. Maybe I could even be a missionary leader for one of these projects.

We're all leaving very early in the morning to head to Quito, so I'd better get to bed. I'm really going to miss Otavalo, but I will definitely come back next year at the same time.

viernes, el 30 de junio, 2000   / **Día 13** /

Today I had to say good-bye to some people on this mission. I cried because it's so hard to say good-bye to all my new friends. We've become so close during this trip. The others leave tomorrow, and I am sure there will be more tears.

After a two-hour bus ride from Otavalo to Quito, we all walked around for a little while, looking at the city and eating at the American restaurants—Burger King, Pizza Hut, or McDonald's. Some returned to the hotel in order to say good-bye, but most of us decided to take a short road trip to the equator.

The equator was amazing! It was surprisingly cold, though. We were up very high, and there were volcanoes with snow on them. It was quite awesome to stand at the centerline of the world.

sábado, el primer de julio, 2000 / **Día 14** /

So this morning, about 4:00, Lili and I woke up
to say good-bye to everyone. After everyone left, we
went back to sleep for a couple of hours.

Then we woke up and, for the rest of the day, we
talked about everything. We talked about the unity of
Christian believers and how even though not everyone
on the team was Christian, we all shared one thing: the
belief in and love of our Father. There were some
people on this trip who did not feel as close as others
to God, but they were not shunned or looked down
upon; everyone was welcomed and loved. We talked
about how we could feel God's presence every day and
in everything we did. His presence was unavoidable.
This trip has shown me how to love God more and see
Him in everything.

I definitely don't want to leave tomorrow. Yes, I
want to see my family and friends, but I don't know
how to prepare for home and the United States.

I am going to bed now for the last time in
Ecuador.

domingo, el 2 de julio, 2000 / **Día 15** /

It was even harder to leave than I'd thought. I
cried when we started flying. Right now I'm dreading
entering the United States. In a couple of hours we

will be in Miami, and I will write more then. I will be out of Ecuador then.

2:00 P.M.

Well, in just an hour and a half, we will be in Newark Airport. I miss people already and am definitely returning to Ecuador as soon as I can.

Chapter 3

john rzeznik:
this DOLL'S LIFE

He grew up with an alcoholic dad, then became an orphan by the age of sixteen. Goo Goo Doll John Rzeznik shares his painful story.

John Rzeznik, as told to Jennifer Graham

First off, I would like to apologize for the oversaturation of "Iris." Although it wasn't the Goo Goo Dolls' first hit—"Name" was, in 1995—it did bring us a giant slice of fame that we never imagined possible.

When my band mates Robby Takac and Mike Malinin and I performed at the American Music Awards in 1999, we found out that we were up for three Grammys. That was insane to me. When I think back on the first half of my thirty-five years on Earth, sometimes I can't believe that I've made it here intact.

I don't want to sound like I'm bitching about my upbringing. Now I understand it was brilliant in many ways. My sisters (Phyllis, Fran, Glad and Kate) and I are so close today because of the tumult at home in our tight-knit working-class neighborhood in Buffalo, New York.

For as long as I can remember, my dad, Joe, divided his time between his clerk job at the post office and local bars like Three Deuces. When he did come home, drunk and depressed, he'd pass out in his chair—or wouldn't even make it that far. Once, when I was about twelve, my sister Kate and I had to drag him inside, take off his clothes and put him to bed. Anyone who doesn't realize that alcoholism is an actual illness—not just some character flaw—never met my father.

During my childhood, he had three heart attacks. A man in his fifties, he was overweight, diabetic, and he smoked and drank whiskey. (To this day, if I smell whiskey on somebody, it sends shivers down my spine.) He just couldn't stop. I hated him for a long time. But I loved my mom, Edith. She played the flute and got us well on our way to reading and writing before the first grade. She took a job as a teacher at my

Catholic grade school, Corpus Christi, so we could go there tuition-free. When I was about seven years old, she turned me on to music—first, accordion lessons, then a few years later, the electric guitar.

My mom was hard on my dad, and there was a serious violent phase in their marriage. He would come home drunk when we were little kids, and they would start fighting. Once when I was fourteen, he hit her, and I punched him so hard in the face that he fell to the floor. But my mother turned on me, hitting me for not respecting my father. It was insane.

I had more than my share to rebel against, so I became a troublemaker. I'd get back at my dad through vandalism (once, in my early teens, I smeared blacktop fluid all over a funeral parlor) and by stealing money from his wallet.

When I became a sophomore at Buffalo's McKinley High School, my already shaky home life completely shattered. At fifty-five, my dad got pneumonia, fell into a diabetic coma and died. My sisters were upset, but I was too angry to grieve. That emotion set in more than a year later, but by then it wasn't for him. As my family was struggling to recover from my dad's death, my mom (who was also overweight and a smoker) died suddenly of a heart attack, at age fifty-three.

It was the most horrifying experience. I remember thinking, What am I going to do? Where am I going to go? I had my sisters, but they were just kids, too. We had no other family.

My sister Phyllis became my legal guardian and found an apartment for me in the neighborhood around Buffalo State College. Glad kept the house; the other two moved in together elsewhere in town. So, at seventeen, I was on my own. With a small, monthly Social Security check from my deceased parents, I budgeted my rent, my grocery bills, my clothes. I was totally self-reliant, but I was also a total wreck—and it showed.

Friends to the Rescue

Throughout high school, I was a punk; I even showed up to gym period in combat boots so I wouldn't have to participate. I was always skipping school—who did I have to answer to? And three or four nights a week, I would drink beer until I blacked out. I was too young to have learned from my father's mistakes.

But this isn't a story of doom and gloom. What happened next is the basis for why I believe in God— or at least, in a greater being than myself. Just as things started to get really dark, somebody was sent into my life to help me. In retrospect, I see there was a plan. You don't make it through a nightmare like mine and end up with this kind of success without figuring that out.

During my sophomore year, Joey O'Grady became my best friend and introduced me to people who were into the same kind of music that I was—punk bands like The Clash, The Damned, the Sex Pistols. I started playing with them in garage bands, and for the first time in my life, I had something I really cared about: songwriting and playing music.

After I graduated from high school, my girlfriend, Laurie Kwasnik, helped me apply to and get in to Buffalo State College. Academia didn't stick—I dropped out after freshman year—but that's when I met another student and musician, Robby Takac. When we were about nineteen, we formed the Goo Goo Dolls (along with then-drummer George Tutuska), taking our name from an advertisement in a magazine.

Coming to Terms

By the time I was twenty, we had a deal with Celluloid, a small label. I wish I could tell young musicians that a record deal equals success, but I can't. The Goo Goo Dolls didn't have a hit for nine years (by then we were with Warner Brothers). We put out five records, went on brutal van tours and did everything we could to keep going. Not to say there weren't good times. In 1990, I met Laurie Farinacci; she became my wife in 1993.

With the double-platinum success of our fifth album, *A Boy Named Goo,* in 1995, we quit our day jobs. After hearing our hit "Name," the music director for the movie *City of Angels* asked us to write a song, which became "Iris." Then, in September 1998, we released our sixth album, *Dizzy Up the Girl.*

Every day I'm reminded of my dad and his alcoholism, and my struggle with his legacy. In every city we play, there's a party. Radio programmers, record executives, friends—everybody wants to buy you a beer. When I was in my teens, I could have drunk them under the table. But I'm ever-conscious of what happened to my dad. When you realize the amount of destruction it can cause not only to yourself but to the people around you, it's, like, why bother?

A few years ago, I visited my dad's sisters, Frances and Irene, in San Diego. They told me something I never knew about my father. They explained that their dad—the grandfather I never knew—died when mine was just nine. He'd owned a bar, and my dad had looked forward to taking over the business. But while my father was in the navy, my grandmother sold the bar, robbing my dad of his dream. They said he was never quite the same after that.

One night, I dreamed that my dad was sitting in his chair, and I whispered in his ear, "I got enough money to buy the bar back." He started laughing. When I woke up, I realized that it was the best closure I could ask for.

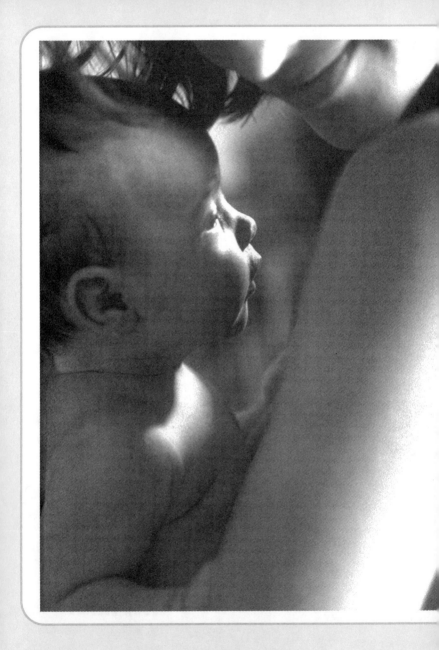

jessica owens*:
soul
SURVIVOR

Like most teens, Jessica Owens* thought more about getting good grades and having lots of friends than she did about God. But when she got pregnant, all that changed.

Jessica Owens*, as told to Megan Howard

My parents got divorced when I was in eighth grade. I was fourteen years old, and we moved from South Jersey up to North Jersey, about fifteen minutes away from Pennsylvania. I had to change schools, but it ended up being okay. I made lots of new friends and I had the perfect little high school life going on. But then my mother and stepfather started having problems. They lost their business and the house, so we

*Not her real name

had to move again. This time to Pennsylvania, where things are less expensive.

I was devastated. I was only fifteen at the time, so I had absolutely no control over where we lived. Pennsylvania was their choice, so that was where I had to live as well. Away from all of my friends in New Jersey, I felt like I had nothing. I became really depressed and cried a lot. I missed home.

I tried to find new friends, but I always felt like the outsider. I just didn't mesh with the kids in my new school. People in Pennsylvania are more reserved than they are in New Jersey, and much more religious. I finally made a couple of good friends, but it still wasn't the same.

When I was a junior in high school, one of my friends asked me to go with her to the prom. She said, "Oh, you have to go to the prom with me. You're my friend and I won't let you stay home." She set me up with her ex-boyfriend, Nick, so I wouldn't be going alone, and Nick and I ended up hitting it off really well. He was so nice. We started dating.

We saw each other as much as we could and talked on the phone every day. Nick was just what I needed at that time. Just by being around, he was helping me out of my depression. I felt like things were finally looking up.

Nick was still in high school, but he was eighteen and didn't live with his parents. Instead, he stayed with his friend, Goey. After we had been dating for a few months, Goey asked Nick to leave, because he couldn't support Nick anymore. My parents, feeling sorry for him and me, let him move in with us. It was perfect. For the first time in a long time I was happy.

Living together brought Nick and me closer. We were falling in love, and we wanted to take our relationship to the next level—so we decided to have sex.

Everything Changes

I know it was a mistake, but Nick and I weren't careful, and I got pregnant. I knew I was pregnant right away, but I didn't want to believe it. I didn't tell anybody. I didn't even take a pregnancy test to confirm what I knew inside. I just couldn't face it. I was doing well in school. I was feeling better about myself. I was happy. I couldn't believe this was happening to me.

When I finally did take a home pregnancy test, about two months after Nick and I had had sex, it came out positive—instantly. All I could think was, Oh, my God. I can't ignore it anymore. I couldn't ignore it, but I still didn't tell my mom.

I did tell Nick, though, and we thought about

getting an abortion. In Pennsylvania you have to be eighteen or have a parent's permission. In New Jersey and Maryland you don't, so we thought about going across the state line and getting one. I'm an impulsive person, but I knew I couldn't go through with something as drastic as an abortion without my mom by my side. So we ditched that plan.

At the time, Nick and I were working at a convenience store down the street from my house, and I confided in a couple of the girls there. One of them decided to call my mom. She told my mom that I was pregnant and that I was thinking about getting an abortion—even though by this time I had decided I wasn't going to go through with it. My mom freaked out. She was really hurt and upset that I hadn't told her. And she was very disappointed that I hadn't been more careful about using birth control. She said that a lot.

My mom went down to the store where Nick and I worked and confronted him. She was yelling at him, as any parent would in that situation. The manager actually had to ask her to leave, and he threatened to call the cops if she didn't. My mom almost kicked Nick out of our house, but then she decided that he should stay around. He'd helped create the situation, so he should have to live with it and help see me through it. So he stayed.

By the time my mom calmed down and we were able to talk rationally about my pregnancy, it was too late to get an abortion. I was about three months' pregnant. We needed to decide what to do, but it was so hard for me to think about it. I was scared. I had had all these big plans for my future, but now none of them could happen.

I knew I had basically two choices: I could keep my baby, or give it up for adoption. If I kept my baby, I couldn't do anything that I had planned. I couldn't go to a college out of state. I would have to live at home, because I would need help taking care of my baby. If I gave it up for adoption, I thought I would have a better life. Nick strongly supported the idea as well. So I looked into it. I called an adoption agency to see how it worked. But I was really torn. I wanted the best for my child, but I also wanted the best for me, and I had a really hard time finding that balance.

As I grew bigger, things became even more difficult. Although I loved school, I didn't want to go anymore. I didn't want to be ridiculed and, as my senior year progressed, I didn't fit in the desks anymore. So my mom made a deal with the principal: Since I had taken a lot of advanced courses and I had enough credits to graduate, he decided it would be okay if I didn't attend school during the second half of my senior year. It was a relief to be able to wait out the end of my pregnancy away from the stares of my classmates, but at the same time it was a lonely existence. I was isolated from the things and people I enjoyed.

I was lost—spiritually and emotionally. And now I had to face this huge decision—whether or not to keep my baby—and I needed to do some real soul-searching. I thought about who I was, now and before I got pregnant, and what kind of person I wanted to be.

The thought of being a mom was terrifying, but my mom helped me see that giving up my baby would be just as hard. Sure, in the short term while I was eighteen, nineteen or twenty, it would make my life easier. But when I thought about the rest of my life, and the rest of my baby's life, I wasn't so sure that being separated from each other was the best choice, either. Adoption was a decision I wouldn't be able to change. I couldn't pull my child out of its life ten years from now. Also, I read an article about people who had given up their kids, and it wasn't as easy as it seemed. This scared me. I didn't think I could live with the guilt.

I finally decided I couldn't give my baby up. I

chose the name Abigail—I didn't even pick out a boy's name—and on March 3, 2000, Abi was born.

New Beginnings

The first time I held Abi in my arms, I said to my mother, "You know what? I get it. I understand the word 'no.' I understand everything you did during my life that I didn't like, and I understand why you did it." All the nos and groundings and moves—all of a sudden I understood, because Abi was more important. I had to take care of her—and protect her. The knowledge that I had the power to make her the most wonderful, kind, loving and strong woman in the world or make her feel like nothing was—*is*—a really big responsibility.

For the first time I was part of something bigger. Life was no longer just about having lots of friends. I was taking care of Abi, but at the same time she was showing me everything there is to life. Even my eating habits changed because of her. Chips and cookies are no longer staples in my diet. I've become a vegetarian. As small as that may seem, it's part of something bigger— shaping her to be the best person I can make her.

Nick stayed with us throughout my pregnancy. But shortly after Abi was born, it became obvious that he wasn't going to help take care of her. We both decided it was time for him to move out. He was also not getting along with my mom because he couldn't live by her rules, so when Abigail was just about three months old, he packed up and left. We haven't seen him since.

Getting over Nick was hard. He wasn't a lot of help when he was there, but it was nice having someone. Now I was back to having nobody, and I didn't want to be alone. But Abi also opened me up spiritually. I started praying for something in my life that would give me the strength to—not go on, because I wasn't going to kill myself—but live without tons of friends. Up until then, all I knew was that if you wanted to have a good life, you needed a lot of friends. Now I needed to find something else that would give me a good life.

I found God. I don't think of Him as a person or being who watches and passes judgment on us. But I know there's something out there and it helps me. I think about Him as a big, powerful force. When I don't have enough energy to do everything that I have to do, He helps me. If I need a pat on the back and nobody's there to give one to me, I can sit down and think and pray, "I really need help. I'm really having trouble here." Then something will happen, like my mom will hand me twenty dollars to go out, and I'll know it happened because I asked for it.

That happens a lot. I'll ask for little things, from helping Abigail get back to sleep at two o'clock in the morning to spending more time with her, to bigger things like having the strength to not let other people's negative opinions about being a young mother bother me.

Without Abi I would have been just another stupid nineteen-year-old doing stupid things. With her I've been forced to grow up. I'm a lot stronger emotionally. And even though physically I'm only nineteen, everything else about me is more like twenty-five or twenty-six. I have to think about things more before I act. I now have to consider whether I want some guy in my life, or if the job that I want to take will interfere too much with my time with Abi. Before her, I didn't think about it. If I wanted something, I would just go out and get it.

I've had people come up to me when I've been walking through the mall. They hand me pamphlets and say, "You can be saved. It's okay that you made this sin." Like my child is some evil devil with horns.

My child is not a devil; she's an angel. She's changed my world in so many ways. She's brought God and faith into my life. Life is still hard, but I know with Abi and with God's help, I'll get through whatever comes my way.

Chapter 5

choosing
my RELIGION

What does spirituality mean to you?
Here's how five teens have made faith a part
of their lives—in very different ways.

Allison Adato

As the oldest of five kids in an Orthodox family in Denver, Abby Calm always took pride in being a religious role model for her siblings. But two years ago she started to reexamine the rules that she had been following so closely. "I needed to come to terms with [Judaism] for myself," she says, "rather than just taking it from my parents." She spent the next two summers studying Judaism in Israel and chose to stick with her faith; she now embraces the direction it gives her life. "It was inspiring to see that there are Jews who live by the letter of the law, where God is the focus of their minds when they make decisions," she says.

In light of her decision, Abby has had to accept the limited role that women traditionally play in the Orthodox faith. Each week, while her father, an ordained rabbi and computer programmer, and her brothers pray in the men's section of the synagogue and read from the Torah (Judaism's holiest text), Abby sits in the women's area with her mother, a Hebrew and Judaic studies teacher, her sisters and female friends. Because she's a girl, Abby isn't allowed to read the Torah or study to become a rabbi. "I don't think God is sexist or that he doesn't like women," she says. "Women are not God's top priority. I don't think telling me that my role isn't to lead a service [means he has] a grudge against females."

Some might say that Abby's faith poses a threat to her social life. Unlike her less devout friends at Rocky Mountain Hebrew Academy, she observes the Sabbath, which occurs year round from sundown Friday to sundown Saturday. During that time she's forbidden to drive or ride in a car, use electricity, watch TV, talk on the phone and listen to the radio—

she can't even do homework.

Still, Abby takes the restrictions in stride. "I have friends who go to the movies on Friday night, but I have other friends who are at services with me," she says. And when her friends eat at non-kosher restaurants? "I go and talk," she says, "I just don't eat." Abby's self-censorship also extends to fashion choices. "There are certain things you [do] to be more modest," she says. "I only wear skirts; I don't wear sleeveless shirts."

Abby knows that her level of devotion isn't for everyone and tries to be open-minded about how others choose to practice. "I have a friend who reads from the Torah. I don't agree with it, but I respect her because she feels so passionately about it," says Abby, who also gives slack to guys she dates. "They have to be Jewish," she says, "but they don't have to be Orthodox."

At school, Marlies Fitch has always been a fierce debater.
Two years ago she used those skills to win her toughest
argument yet—at home. After visiting a Methodist
church with friends, Marlies was moved to convince her
parents that they should go there instead of attending
the family's regular Catholic church. "I hated the way
the Catholic church taught us," says the Texan. "It was
like they were throwing religion at me. At the Methodist

church, they'd be, like, 'God is a cool person; God will forgive you if you do something bad.'"

Amazingly, her parents, both lifelong Catholics, gave in. And that's when religion became a major part of Marlies's busy life—one that was already jam-packed with debate tournaments, local theater performances and beauty pageants (she was fourth runner-up in the 1998 Miss Teen Texas America competition). "It's kind of popular to be a Christian now. People go to church and wear the 'What Would Jesus Do?' bracelets like it's a fashion statement," says Marlies, who scoffs at the trend. "But after a while, you see who's really devoted to Christ."

Like Marlies, many of the devoted are members of the Christian Student Union and the Fellowship of Christian Athletes, religious clubs that meet at The Woodlands High School. Because they aren't part of the official classroom curriculum, these clubs don't cross the legal line separating church and state. It's a division Marlies has learned to respect, ever since she was sent to detention during junior high school for bringing a Bible to study hall and reading to a group of interested students. But because the Methodist brand of Christianity considers evangelism (spreading the word of Jesus Christ) an important tenet, Marlies still tries to talk to people about Jesus whenever she can. "If my best friend is an atheist, I'm not going to see her in Heaven," she says. "I just have to think that I've done all I can do."

That includes confronting peers who smoke or drink, singing gospel songs during pageant talent segments as well as holding prayer circles backstage. Even so, honoring her beliefs while fulfilling her pageant duties isn't always easy. "Sometimes on stage I feel like a piece of meat," says Marlies. "Showing your body is sexual. I just try to forget about it and say, 'Hey, I'm singing to God. I'll be fine.'"

Marlies also puts her values to the test on the dating scene. "People have challenged me on the subject of sex," she admits. But so far, she's stuck to her beliefs: "Everything—from hanging out with friends to the music you listen to—it all comes down to what you believe in."

Hakim Muhammad, Muslim

Hakim Muhammad is a lot like his friends in the Boston area. He hangs out, plays basketball and rides around the neighborhood on his bike. One thing, however, does set him apart: He hasn't met one other Muslim at Blue Hills Regional Technical School in Canton, Massachusetts.

Hakim's classmates, most of whom are Christian, have always been curious about his faith, Islam.

Especially when it comes to Ramadan, the holy period when Muslims everywhere fast from sunrise to sundown every day for a full month. "I like explaining it to other people," says Hakim. "We get up before sunrise and eat a little, maybe a peanut butter and jelly sandwich or a bagel and some water. It says in the Koran [the sacred text of Islam] that fasting will give you blessings, that it's a good deed." Of course, doing the right thing sometimes takes superhuman willpower: "Like at school," says Hakim, "when everybody's eating in front of my face."

Muslims are required to pray five times a day, and the men, specifically, must go to the *masjid*, or mosque, their place of worship, every Friday for services. But it's not always possible to meet those demands. "Sometimes my mom won't go to the *masjid* because she has to work," says Hakim. "We all try to go every Friday afternoon, but I don't go [as often] during the school year, because it would be taking up class time. What's important is to do the best you can."

Hakim often finds himself explaining his religion to people around him, which he thinks is in part due to the fact that there aren't many famous American role models who are practicing Muslims. "There's Hakeem Olajuwon," says Hakim, referring to the center for the Houston Rockets basketball team, whom he admires. "During Ramadan, Hakeem plays ball, gets sweaty and doesn't even have a drink. I know people ask him questions, but he just stays strong."

Before Hakim was born, his parents converted from Christianity to Islam and changed their last name to the more traditional Muslim name of Muhammad. Occasionally, Hakim has felt as if he's missed out because of that decision. "One time, I wanted some gummi bears," he says. "But my mom said no, because there's pork in the gelatin and we're not supposed to eat pork." Another time, he wanted to go to the movies during Ramadan, but his father refused to let him because each Muslim is encouraged to read the entire Koran, which is roughly six hundred pages, during that month. But as he has grown older, Hakim has learned to love the faith and even appreciate its restrictions. "I was born a Muslim," he says. "My parents do it, so now it's time for me to do it, too."

Dominic Manzanares,

Buddhist

"I grew up Catholic, going to church every Sunday," says Dominic Manzanares. "I enjoyed it for a long time, but by the time I was ready for confirmation, I was looking into different things." Dominic was then fourteen and struggling with problems: There were pressures at school, fights on the streets of his hometown, Espanola, New Mexico, and growing tension between him and his mom (his parents divorced when he was an infant). Unable to cope, Dominic ran away—the first of many such flights.

Over the next year, Dominic's problems only got

worse. By the time he was fifteen, he was experimenting with crank, or methamphetamine, and facing a weapons possession and assault charge resulting from an argument that broke out on a hunting trip. Fortunately, the charges were dropped, and after about five months, Dominic stopped doing drugs. But he needed to make a bigger change.

Soon after, at sixteen, he quit school and went to work with an older friend installing satellite dishes. "He was practicing Hinduism," says Dominic of his friend, "and he taught me some basic yoga. I started practicing and felt a lot better." That inspired Dominic to explore other religions. He began looking at *Tricycle*, a Buddhist magazine, and reading books on everything from philosophy to magic. But it was a Buddhist poem, "Call Me By My True Name," that really hit home. "It's about being who you are," he says, "and taking responsibility for who you are."

A devout Catholic, Dominic's mother was mystified—and miffed—that he was opening himself up to new faiths. "My mom thought I was going insane because of the things I was talking about," he says. "She wanted me to talk to the priest and was [considering] turning me over to the state, because she couldn't control me. I needed to go somewhere."

He sought refuge at the Hidden Mountain Zen

Center, a Buddhist temple in Albuquerque, where he began practicing intensive meditation for eight hours a day. "I sat for four days," he says, still amazed by his own discipline. "You go through all your thoughts in your mind. A lot of memories came up that were hard, but the practice is to just let it go. That's the first couple of days. Then you get really, really uncomfortable. Even during breaks, there's no talking. You sit in the morning, eat breakfast, work a couple of hours, then start sitting again."

In the past two years, Dominic has returned to the temple for several more of these four-day retreats, or "sesshins"—once even bringing his mother along. The visit helped convince her that the Buddhist teachings had been good for Dominic, who finally decided to buckle down and finish high school (he graduated in June 1998).

Today, Dominic's found the balance between his old and new faiths: He's a practicing Buddhist who still believes in Christ. "I guess I'm a Zen Catholic," he says. Even more important is the lesson he learned on his religious search. "I don't want to hurt people anymore. And I don't want to be hurt," he says. "I see [people] put on an act just to fit in. But if you talk to them, you bring out the real person inside. I'm trying to help people through things I was once struggling with."

"To me, religion is my own personal set of beliefs," says Laura Stinger. "It doesn't have anything to do with a god." Her father's family is Christian; her mother was born Jewish. But Laura wasn't raised in either of those religions. She'd go to church with her grand-parents once in a while, and she thought of holidays like Hanukkah and Christmas as times when she could "see the family and, like, eat a lot."

57

Laura's the first to admit that she has real doubts about whether or not God exists, but she does still wonder about some of religion's larger questions: What is our purpose in life? What are we on this earth for? Laura figures it's "for something bigger than getting a job or going to school—something that will make your life a journey with meaning."

Looking to start her own life's journey, Laura deferred college for a year and arranged to take a five-month solo trip to Nepal, a South Asian country where Buddhism and Hinduism are practiced. Laura found information on the Internet about educational work being done in a Nepalese village and contacted the organizers to volunteer. "In Katmandu, everyone talks about everything," she says. "I had great talks about spirituality that had nothing to do with religion. I was having tea with the guy who owned the motel where I was staying, and we talked about whether good and evil really exist; about true love and partners for life. For me, that's what spirituality is: the deep questions you ask yourself and how you act on those."

Laura has found some of the answers, but is still searching for others. "My definition of reli-

gion is that it's about having your own sensors,"
says Laura. "It's your heart, the way you live. You
have to know your inner core before you can apply
things from a book."

Chapter 6

leah sell:
SO MOTE
IT BE

Leah Sell not only found her religion, she chose it over her family and friends.

Leah Sell, as told to Megan Howard

Different from the Rest

I'm basically a normal teenager, but I have done something most people my age haven't: I have converted religions and found my true faith, Wicca. Looking at me you'd never think I was a witch, but I am. No, I don't dress in all black or sacrifice living things, but I believe in the nature-based Spirit, composed of the Lord and Lady to whom all Wiccans pray.

Finding My Religion

I was brought up by my father in the Catholic religion, but had never agreed with it. I always thought there were both male and female parts to a superior being and I believed in reincarnation. I had also always been drawn to witchcraft but had thought it to be more like magic or illusions.

In the summer of 1999 I was in a very depressed state. As I strolled through the young adult section of a bookstore one day, my hand fell upon a book called *Teen Witch*. I begged my father to buy it for me, trying my hardest not to let him know what it was about. After some bargaining, he bought it and I spent the entire weekend reading it. At first I was a bit disappointed to find that becoming a witch would not give me amazing abilities of power overnight, but then I learned what it *would* give me. I found out it was a religion that was actually very down-to-earth and focused more on nature than on black magic. All summer my interest in the Wicca religion grew, and I studied anything I could get my hands on.

The Choice: Family or Faith

When school started back up, my beliefs were challenged. I was taking religious classes in preparation for my confirmation in the Catholic

Church. Even though I still didn't agree with my father's religion, there was no way I could get out of this important sacrament. I couldn't talk to my dad about my new religion because whenever I tried to bring it up, he would either make fun of it or bombard me with questions about Wicca. There was no way that I could tell my whole family that I was converting over to another religion. I just couldn't deal with that much.

I was so depressed and stressed out about everything, I was very near suicide. I had failed a test in school, my friends were blowing me off, and not only were things rough with my dad, I wasn't getting along with my mother very well, either. Even though my mom isn't a religious person, she was pushing me to agree with my father and go through with the sacrament. She didn't understand that because I was being forced to take confirmation classes, I was betraying not only my own new religion, but also the Catholic Church that I had been raised in. I was at the point where I thought, Nothing is going to get better. This is how it's been forever, and this is how it's going to be. Let's just end it.

I sat there looking at my wrists and thought about how a few seconds of physical pain could end a lifetime of physical, mental and spiritual pain. I just sat there thinking and crying. Then I remembered a Wiccan principle: Life on earth is like a classroom, and you will continue to be reincarnated until you've learned all of life's lessons, then you will get to rest with the Spirit. I thought to myself, I've already spent thirteen years here. Even if I die now, I'm going to have to come back, anyway, so I might as well get as much as I can out of this life. I talked to the Wiccan Spirit and I prayed to the Lord and Lady. They gave me an inner power, and a voice within me kept saying, "You can't do this. This isn't what's supposed to happen. You can't go through with the confirmation." My Wiccan beliefs gave me a beautiful gift of strength. I owe my life to my faith.

Now that I knew I couldn't be confirmed in the Catholic Church, I had to figure out a way to get out of it—or at least make it right with myself and my own religion. Before I was confirmed, I had to go to confession and meet with a priest. While the priest was blessing me, I said (in my head) to the Catholic God, "Thank you for the knowledge and the kindness that this parish has shown me, but I'm moving on and I hope you will accept that. I hope you will not hold any grudges against me or my family for my choice and my new belief." After that, I felt everything was going to be okay.

Dealing with Opposition

Then, things at school got bad again. During my freshman year, I decided to start wearing my pentacle ring. It symbolizes the Wiccan religion, and my decision to wear it announced my commitment to my beliefs. My mom told me not to wear it because she thought it would only cause trouble, but I told her I was proud of my religion and I would never hide it. "Everyone else gets to wear crosses around their neck," I said. "Why can't I wear my pentacle on my finger?"

At first, no one really noticed anything. Then, about two weeks after I started wearing it, the girl sitting next to me in civics class asked, "You're not into witchcraft and that kind of stuff, are you?" I told her, "I've been a witch since the middle of summer before eighth grade. You know, nothing has changed." But she told me I was different now. There were some boys sitting behind us and I guess they heard us talking, because they started chanting softly, "Witch, witch, witch." I don't mind being called that, because that's what I am, but their tone of voice was so mean and accusing. One of my friends was sitting nearby and heard the boys. She had never heard me say a word about witchcraft before, but I guess she figured out that since I was wearing my pentacle ring and talking about Wicca, something was going on. Then someone asked me for a piece of gum, and my friend said in the most coldhearted voice, "You don't want that. That's witch gum. It's evil." I knew prejudice and ignorance existed, but I had never really experienced them before. Since then, I have learned who my real friends are.

I have been called a devil worshiper and a Satanist so many times. It's exhausting having to deny rumors about myself and defend Wicca all the time. I don't mind, though, because I would rather have to explain my religion four hundred times over than have people go around making up things about me that aren't true. Some people won't listen to my explanations and they still believe the rumors, but at least I have tried to offer them some knowledge.

Coming to Terms with Being Different

Wicca has allowed me to find a faith where everything I believe in is accepted. I've made new friends and become more open-minded. Because I constantly have to defend my faith, I've had to become more out-going and strong. I have finally found something I strongly believe in. And I am glad.

Chapter 7

julie stoffer:
keeping the
FAITH

The Real World cast member Julie Stoffer tells the real story behind her university suspension and how it's affected her family, her future and her Mormon faith.

Julie Stoffer, as told to Jon Barrett

In July 2000 I was in Montreal taping MTV's *Real World/Road Rules Challenge* when officials at Brigham Young University in Provo, Utah, turned my life upside down. They informed me that I had broken the Mormon church–owned school's honor code—which forbids unrelated members of the opposite sex to live together—by being on *The Real World New Orleans* earlier that year. The punishment was one year's suspension. When I first heard the news I went through a series of emotions: confusion, anger, depression. But now, as I'm rebuilding my life in Southern California, I realize that BYU's decision was nothing less than a blessing.

I grew up in Delafield, Wisconsin, the oldest of five kids in a strict Mormon household. Mormonism emphasizes living a "chaste and virtuous life." Alcohol, tobacco and caffeinated drinks, like tea and coffee, are banned, and premarital sex and homosexuality are considered sins. The church enforces its tenets in a very all-or-nothing fashion. I would get up at four A.M. every weekday to drive forty-five minutes to attend seminary classes with ten other Mormon teens, and one Saturday night a month my family would drive an hour and a half to attend church dances with other Mormon families in the region. In high school I clung to my Mormon friends because I didn't think I had much in common with the kids at my school. I would say to myself, "Someday I'm going to BYU, and everyone will be Mormon and it will be my Zion, my paradise."

Paradise Lost

I started my freshman year at BYU in 1997. BYU is a fine institution of learning, but it's basically white

Mormon kids with very high grade point averages. By my junior year I yearned to meet different kinds of people and explore more of the world around me. One day in October 1999, a friend showed me an article in the student paper announcing that MTV was holding a local casting call for *The Real World*. I didn't know much about the show; my parents never allowed MTV in our home because they believed it wasn't consistent with the church's values. Curious, I agreed to join my friend at the event the next day. My casting interview lasted only five minutes, so I didn't really expect to hear about *The Real World* again. To my total surprise they called me back, and I had several more interviews over the next couple of months. But it wasn't until the semifinals in November 1999, when MTV flew me to Los Angeles (my first time on an airplane), that I thought, Dude, this might happen. After I returned to Utah, I thought, If three days in L.A. was that cool, I want to do five months in New Orleans.

I started telling classmates about the possibility of my doing the show, and began to realize how big a deal this would be at BYU, where having an "extreme" hairstyle or wearing shorts above the knee are considered honor-code violations. My roommates called house meetings to discuss how any affiliation with the network was a bad idea. Guys I didn't know approached me on campus and said it was their "priesthood obligation" to discourage me from being on the show. I even got called into my bishop's office twice.

After I finally got the call from MTV in mid-December, I asked someone in the honor-code office what would happen if I went on the show. I was told that they couldn't make a decision until they watched it and discussed it with me.

But my biggest worry at that time was telling my parents that I planned to take a semester off from school to do *The Real World*. I've always had a big thing about not pleasing my dad—that I didn't live up to his idea of the perfect daughter—so I had decided to keep the audition a secret. When the moment of truth arrived, I tried to break it to my dad easily, but he practically had a heart attack. He had a friend tape past episodes of the show and he pointed out all the things cast members did that were morally wrong and why I shouldn't do it. I totally understood where he was coming from. Going against his wishes was hard—but I knew I was going to do this, and I knew he didn't like it.

Wake-Up Call

The five months I spent having my life taped twenty-four hours a day in New Orleans were like shell shock. On *The Real World* I was the "Molly

Mormon" girl who'd never realized how much of the world she hadn't been exposed to. And I didn't know how ignorant I sounded until I started watching the show. I remember how I would throw the word "colored" around when talking about African Americans. But now, especially after meeting my *Real World* housemate Melissa, who's both Filipino and black, I realize how offensive that word can be. After watching those first episodes I called the director and cried. But he just said, "Julie, that's the way you were."

Everyone has their catalyst, their getting-away-from-home, getting-away-from-the-comfortable experience. Mine just happened to take place on national television. When you think about it, everyone in *The Real World* house was naive. Each of us had grown up in our own little bubble.

Danny, who's openly gay, was as naive to my Mormonism as I was to his homosexuality. Even though I had been taught that homosexuality is wrong, it wasn't until I met Danny that I realized I had no right to judge someone's sexuality. It's no one's business but his own. I hope people who watch the show see that I've learned to live by the principles behind the rules I've followed my whole life, and not just by the rules themselves. I'm proof that you can live with guys and still be chaste and virtuous. I believe in abstinence, but not only because I believe in God. I don't know how I would react if I were in a sexually active relationship that ended, so I want to wait until I'm married. In this case, the reason behind sticking to the rule is simply knowing what's best for me.

I got home from New Orleans in June and started sharing what I had learned with my four brothers and sisters. This upset my parents, especially my dad, who made it clear that he didn't want me to live at home that summer if I was going to continue "putting thoughts," especially about homosexuality, into my siblings' heads. By that time, however, I'd been selected to go on *The Real World/Road Rules Challenge* starting in July.

"Don't go," my dad pleaded. I didn't want to dig him an early grave by adding to his stress. But this was an awesome, once-in-a-lifetime opportunity. I couldn't keep living my life according to my father's expectations. I was the navigator of my own destiny.

I had been struggling with whether to return to BYU in September, because I hadn't been happy there. But at that point, I was planning to go back—it was affordable, and I looked forward to joining my brother Alan on campus.

I didn't think BYU would refuse to take me back. I called the school three times during *The Real World* taping, but they said they didn't want to go into the situation in depth because all phone conversations were recorded for the show. When I spoke to an honor-code official after I got home to Wisconsin, he asked me if I'd had sex or any other physical contact with my room-mates. I told him that I hadn't done anything I was ashamed of. A few weeks later the same school official called to tell me he wanted to fly out to Wisconsin to "review" the situation. I told him that it was too late—I was leaving for the Challenge the following day.

The next thing I knew I was reading a letter informing me I'd been suspended. When I saw the official reason—"for your relationship with members of the opposite sex, specifically sleeping together with them on multiple occasions"—I was furious. I felt as if they were accusing me not only of living with men but of having sex with them! I wanted to shout, "Okay, you kicked me out! But don't ruin my reputation while you're at it." Sure, I would lie in the same bed as Danny, but there was never anything inappropriate about our relationship. I'm still a virgin, and I have the videotape to prove it.

I don't know if this will end up on the Challenge, but after being suspended I kind of went crazy. I had a little nervous breakdown because there was just too much pressure: from the school, the media, the show—and all the while, I was being filmed by a crew that wanted to catch every emotion. I would just sit on the bus and not talk with anyone. I was so rude, so competitive. I almost became a different person. I was pretty depressed for a couple of weeks, but the demanding challenges, which included bungee jumping through fire and Indy-style car racing, helped me break out of my funk. They gave me something to focus on besides myself.

A Blessing in Disguise

Ironically, the suspension helped mend my relationship with my dad. After the story hit the news, he felt he needed to defend my character, and he started writing angry letters to the school. He even told the press that I had served the equivalent of a mission for the church by being on the show. My family and the Mormon Church will always be constants in my life. We might have our differences of opinion, but I've learned to live with them and not let them eat me up. In the end, that's why BYU's decision is a blessing. I had planned on returning to the school because I didn't have the guts to do otherwise. Instead, I'm living in California, free to pursue my interests and finish my degree at a new university. I've designed my own Web site and I'm going to take classes in video editing, a passion I discovered while working at the public-access station in New Orleans.

My parents are very accepting of me now. They even have MTV in the house! But my dad is still uncomfortable with my living in California, because he thinks I'm going to have trouble finding a good Mormon boy to marry. In Mormonism, if you're not married in the temple, your family can't be joined for eternity in a ceremony the church calls "sealing." He says, "Julie, we don't want to lose you." And I tell him, "Dad, I'm always going to be there. I'll always be your daughter."

Chapter 8

willa ford:
facing the
MUSIC

Rumors and accusations on the World Wide Web threatened to destroy Willa Ford's career before it even began. Here, Willa talks about how she found the strength to confront—and win over—her accusers.

Willa Ford, as told to Jon Barrett

I've always found a lot of truth in the statement that there's a thin line between love and hate. But it wasn't until August 2000, when I came face-to-face with a girl who hated me without ever having met me before, that I realized how thin that line could be.

I've wanted to be a singer my whole life, and I've
spent years and years of blood, sweat and tears to make
this dream come true. This is just who I am. In fact, if
I didn't have my record deal with Lava/Atlantic, I would
be the kind of person who was living out of her car
touring the country with a jazz band. That could have
been me. But after I started dating Nick Carter from
the Backstreet Boys in 1998, I began getting less attention for my singing and more for being the pop singer
with the most Web sites dedicated *against* her.

I first became aware of the Web craziness in 1999
when my best friend, Kevin, called me up and said,
"Oh, my God, you've got to get on the computer.
There's a girl who's going on the Internet and posting
really bad things about you." After checking it out, I
learned that some people very close to Nick had tried to
hurt him and our relationship by posting a letter on the
Net that he had supposedly written. The letter outlined
ways I had supposedly hurt Nick, including being physically abusive to him and stealing his big-screen TV.

I could tell right away that the letter was a fake—
and not only because everything in it was a lie. Nobody
in the world knows Nick better than I do, and I knew
he wouldn't write something like this. Nevertheless,

what started out as an isolated attempt to hurt Nick sparked more than sixty anti-Willa Web sites—all before I had even released my first album. The girls launching these sites just wigged out—saying, among other things, that I had bruised and slapped Nick, yelled at his fans and kidnapped his dog. As crazy as the sites were, at first I thought they were kind of funny. But when some of them started a boycott against my record company and then went so far as to suggest that I kill myself—I realized this was serious stuff.

Hiding the Pain

It was seriously painful, too. Eventually the sites knocked me into such a deep depression that I could hardly function. Everything was tumbling down around me, I couldn't eat and I lost a lot of weight. I tried to act like I was good to go, but it must have been obvious that I wasn't. Daily doses of Paxil and Xanax helped me through my struggles, but it was the tremendous support from my family, friends and fans that really kept me going. When Kevin wasn't coming over to my house to feed me pizza because he was worried I wasn't eating enough, I was hearing from fans about how inspiring it was that I was working through all the negative attention.

Taking a Stand

So I tried to focus on the fans in the summer of 2000, when I went on a concert tour sponsored by Nautica. At one of the performances a fan warned me that the front row of the audience was filled with anti-Willa people. I did my best to keep it out of my mind. "I don't have time for this right now," I told myself. "I've got fans here and that's all that matters."

When I finished signing autographs after the concert, I noticed one of the girls from the front row standing there staring at me. This time I couldn't push her out of my mind. So I stared back, giving her one of my best "What, do you have a problem with me?" looks. It must have worked, because she came over and started shouting in my face, saying, "You did this, and you did that," basically repeating all the lies on the Web sites.

Before she could finish and walk away, I said, "Listen, I want to sit down and talk with you. I don't understand why everybody hates me. Maybe you can help me out." And that's what we did—we just sat there talking, telling each other our side of the story. She was really mean to me in the beginning, but the conversation started to turn around when I explained how everything had started with the fake letter. Believe it or not, by the time we were done talking, she'd promised to take her anti-Willa site down and replace it with a fan site.

"It's going to take time for all the other girls to understand, and they're not going to believe me when I tell them," she told me. "But when they do realize that they've spent all this time pitting themselves against you because of lies, they're going to want to spend three times that to do positive things for you."

The Beat Goes On

So that's why I say there's a thin line between love and hate, and why I now realize that I am steadily on that line. It's up to me to change the balance. On one side I've got my parents, who are so proud of what I've accomplished; my friends, who often try to come up with ideas for Web sites about how cool I am; my fans, who are simply the best; and God, who gave me the ability to sing. On the other I have the anti-Willa girls. They may want to do whatever they can to end my career, but I've got God on my side. Beyoncé Knowles of Destiny's Child once said that the minute you start thinking you're the bomb and stop thanking God for the gifts He's given, He takes those gifts away. Well, I thank God every day, and I know He's watching over me. Only by continuing to sing can I eventually convince these girls—just like I did with the girl on the Nautica tour—who the real Willa is.

Chapter 9

craig scott:
remembering
RACHEL

As the killers attacked the students in the library at Columbine High School, Craig Scott, sixteen, lay motionless near the body of his friend Isaiah Shoels. Playing dead saved Craig's life. His sister Rachel, seventeen, was not as fortunate. Here, Craig tells how he's struggling to cope with her death.

Craig Scott

I've had a hard time trying to deal with what happened. At times I've felt like I was lost. I've been sad, numb, depressed, angry. But we've had support from a lot of people, and that has really helped. Now I want to make something good come out of this. That's the best thing I can do for Rachel.

It helped to talk with a counselor and a

psychologist. At first, I thought that idea was kind of lame. I thought just talking about it wasn't going to do anything. But it did. It helped in a different way when they gave me a plastic bat and said I could beat on a chair. That got the anger out.

I was angry at Eric and Dylan because my sister was not the sort of person who was an enemy to anybody. They felt no one accepted them, and they watched their Hitler tapes and played Doom to build up all that hate inside them. But Rachel accepted everybody for who they were. She never made fun of anybody. She was just the kind of person they needed, and they shot her.

I can't change what Eric and Dylan did. But maybe I can do something about the way we treat guys like them. The kids who taunted them, who slammed them against lockers, need to change. They need to see that it's not cool to put other people down for a cheap laugh. Nobody really respects that, even though people may not speak up because they're afraid to seem uncool. We need to reach out to kids who seem like they're having problems. We need to find some common ground with them. That's my main goal.

The greatest comfort I have is seeing that some people are trying to be more sensitive to other kids. There's this one big football player at school—his name is Joe—and he wrote me a letter that was totally not what I would have expected from him. He told me he was praying for me, and he said some real nice things. That meant a lot to me. I looked at it and I thought, Wow, he really wrote that with his heart.

I know what happened at Columbine has brought up a lot of issues about schools, families, laws, video games and music. All of the violence that comes at us all the time has to have an effect. You can't pretend that it doesn't, especially on people who aren't real stable. But I honestly don't think that new laws about guns or more metal detectors at school are the answer. They're not going to stop the sort of people who decide to do something like what happened at our school. What we need is a better way of thinking about one another. We need to be more careful about how we treat people who seem torn up inside.

Rachel was such a good example of how to treat people. She was never fake. She was so real with people that everyone respected her. Rachel was her own person. I think of those funny hats she liked to wear: a top hat, a fedora, a sailor hat, a Dr. Seuss hat. When she wore her floppy bucket hat, we called her Gilligan.

I don't want to sound like everything was perfect. We fought sometimes, and we could be bratty to each other. But she was a really good person who was passionate about so many things. She wanted to be a poet, an actress; she wanted to do missionary work. Rachel was secure with who she was. She was pretty, but she wasn't vain. She cut her hair short and dyed it maroon to get into her role in the school play. She played someone who was kind of freaky and looked different but was really a caring person underneath. The play was staged just a couple of weeks before she died.

I keep thinking about an assignment she did for photography class. She took a picture of her hand and wrote a religious poem around it with lots of warm colors. "What if you were to die today. . . . Tomorrow is not a promise but a chance."

I thought it was brave of Rachel to be so real with her classmates about her spiritual feelings. I don't think I'd have the nerve to do it.

I think it's good that people from around the world have poured out their feelings for Rachel and everyone else who got hurt that day. Her car was parked near the school for weeks, covered with things that people left there. It was like a memorial to her, with flowers and wreaths, stuffed animals, balloons, drawings, poems and posters signed by lots of people. My younger brother, Michael, kept some of the things and put them on a table in his room, alongside pictures of Rachel.

It's like his shrine to his big sister.

I know I have to move on eventually because I'll go crazy if I don't. But I don't want to forget Rachel. I want her memory to be strong. I want it to mean a lot. She wanted to reach out, to minister to people with her life. Now she's touching a lot of people with her death.

Chapter 10

jennifer howitt:
hoop
DREAMS

She was your average active kid until a terrible fall left her paralyzed from the chest down. But because of her faith in herself, what could have been a devastating situation opened up a world of opportunity for this West Coast teen.

Jennifer Howitt, as told to Megan Howard

I will never forget the day I hiked up Mount Diablo. It was the summer between third and fourth grade. I was at summer camp. And it was the last time I used my legs.

I don't remember exactly what happened. We were hiking around this spot called Rock City. I lost my footing and fell. I only fell about seven or eight feet, but somehow I landed in a way that broke two vertebrae and crushed my spinal cord. I also broke a wrist and bit my tongue off.

They had to airlift me off the mountain. When you have an accident like this, your body goes into shock, and your mind says weird things. When my mom came to the hospital and I saw her in the emergency room, the first thing I said to her was, "I'm sorry," like I had done this on purpose.

The doctors told us that I had completely severed my spinal cord from T-3/4 level, which is about mid-chest level. That means I have no feeling or movement in my legs from that point down. They did surgery right away and put rods in my back. I then had to spend three months in the hospital going to rehab and getting used to using a wheelchair. It was the worst time of my life.

When I went home, nothing was the same. We had to move to a new house, because our old one had stairs. When I went to school, the bathroom wasn't wheelchair accessible, so they had to change the bathroom for me. They had to prepare all the students for my return, because they had known me how I was before, and now I was different.

I knew I was different—from who I had been

before the accident, and from everyone else. But every time I did anything or went anywhere, my differences were thrown back in my face. I could never forget it, not even for a second. For two years I felt that way, in the fourth and fifth grades. Those were tough times.

She's Got Game

Before my accident, I had played soccer. I was really into sports. So after my accident, my dad decided to take me to a wheelchair tennis tournament. He thought that if I could find something—anything—that I had done before the accident and could do again now, then maybe I would be happier. He was right. I watched the people play, and it dawned on me: Wow! I could do that. That would be kind of fun. I want to play. We did a little investigating and discovered a program called BORP, which stands for Bay Area Outreach and Recreation Program. They organize all sorts of sports for disabled people. So my dad took me to basketball practice. I wasn't quite ready for it. The first time I went, this guy, who I'm now really good friends with, flipped me over backwards in my wheelchair and said, "Welcome to BORP." I was thinking, I do not want to be here. All these people are in wheelchairs. I'm not like that. They're all weird and I don't want to be here. I went home and I didn't go back.

After I spent another year depressed, my dad decided it was time to try again. This time, the people at BORP gave me a basketball right away. I took a shot, and I haven't stopped playing since. When I started playing, I could see that this was a sport. A lot of people think of wheelchair basketball as a disabled sport 'cause it has the word "wheelchair" in the title, but it's a real sport like any other sport. If you're a cyclist, your equipment is your bike. If you play wheelchair basketball, your equipment is your wheelchair. So when I got into it, I realized that I could still play sports. I could still be competitive. I could still train and lift weights and go as far as I wanted to with it.

When I play basketball, I feel as if I'm living in a whole other world. I don't really think about everything else that's going on in life. There's just basketball. The fact that I'm in a wheelchair isn't important. Playing on the BORP team I developed not only as a basketball player, but I also became a stronger person inside—I became a leader. By the time I graduated from high school, I was the captain of the team and we were going to the national championship.

Doing It

I am an athlete. I went to the Olympics in Sydney in 2000. I've competed at the highest level you can. But in school—junior high and high school—I was never considered an athlete. In gym class, when we did sports that I couldn't do, like soccer, I would hold people's stuff, watching from the sidelines. Sometimes I would ask to go to the library so I could do my homework. I didn't want to have to sit there, just watching. It was so frustrating. I felt, like, I'm an athlete. I'm a better athlete than most of these people. I just play a different sport.

Outside of school, my life was completely different. Basketball dominated my life. During high school I played with two teams, the local junior team, the Bay Cruisers, and the women's team, the Bay Area Meteorites. I went to nationals with both teams. My teammates became like my brothers and sisters. When I was with them it was so nice that the wheelchair wasn't an issue or, if it was, it was an issue for all of us. If there was a flight of stairs, then we all had to deal with it.

In 1998, I decided to try out for the women's national team, just for the experience of trying out. I knew in the future that potentially I could be on the team, so I wanted to see what the tryouts were like. But I really didn't think I would make it. I was shocked when they called my name as an alternate. This meant I would train with the team all year but I wouldn't go to the tournament unless someone was injured. I didn't care if I played or not. Just being a part of the team was amazing enough.

I trained all year with the U.S. Women's Wheelchair Basketball Team. I went to all the training camps even though I didn't go to the actual competitions. Still, I grew a whole bunch as a player. Just being involved with the team at such a young age was a big deal. I got some incredible coaching and I got to see how the national team worked, and I'm sure that my year as an alternate helped me make the team in 1999. It's the highest level that you can go to in wheelchair basketball—and I had made it.

You have to try out every year at the national tournament, so I tried out again in 2000. I was selected for that team, too, and I was off to Sydney.

The Paralympics' international governing body is the International Paralympic Committee, which is parallel to the IOC, the International Olympic Committee. The Paralympics are held in the same city as the Olympics, about two weeks later. Athletes stay in the Olympic Village and play in the same venues the Olympic athletes do. We played at the Sydney SuperDome.

I guess because it's a smaller country and because they've had a lot of success in disabled sports, in Australia the Paralympics are almost as big a deal as the Olympics. The SuperDome was a huge venue, and all our games were sold out. Anywhere you went during the Paralympics, it was packed. You'd go to the track and it was packed. One day while we were on the bus on our way to the SuperDome we looked down the main walkway through Olympic Park and it was filled with thousands and thousands of people.

At night they had an hour of TV coverage and they had to increase it to an hour and a half because the public wanted to see more of it. It was interesting, because I went to Atlanta in 1996 to watch all the people that were where I wanted to be, and it wasn't nearly as big a deal. It was barely televised at all.

Even Sydney was barely televised in the United States. But other countries think it's a bigger deal. I have a friend in Japan who saw me on TV.

We actually had an awful tournament and we finished fifth when we should have medaled. But it was still an amazing experience.

Finding Faith

I know a ridiculous number of people now through all the teams and all the tournaments and all the stuff that I've done. I've played on national teams and I've been to Australia four times because of sports. And really that has been the most important thing about sports. They have made me who I am. Regardless of what place we finished in Australia, I'm the person I am today and I've lived the life I've lived, which I love, because of all that's happened—because I fell off that mountain, because I've met these people, because I've played all these games and trained. Basketball showed me that I could live the same life I could have lived before my accident—that a disability just means you do things differently.

Through all of this I've learned you have to have faith that whatever path you're on is the right one. If it feels good to you—if it's what's inside of you and what you want to be doing—then you're going in the right direction regardless of what happens. And, yeah, bad stuff's going to happen, but that's what makes the good stuff happen, too.

j.s.:
a change
of FAITH

She was raised Jewish, but this teen has discovered her faith lies in mankind.

J.S., as told to Megan Howard

Although I am an atheist and do not believe in God, it doesn't mean I don't have faith. I put my faith in my fellow man—despite the Columbine shootings, corrupt politicians, and mothers who drown their children in cars, I still believe that mankind, by nature, is truly good and seeks to help. People have proven this to me again and again.

In my freshman year of high school, I decided

that I was an atheist. I was born Jewish, and I still consider myself Jewish, but it's more a cultural thing than about religion or faith. There wasn't a big event that sparked my change of faith. I was just doing a lot of thinking about creation and the world and history and I realized that I didn't believe there was a God. I realized that religion was invented as a way for people to explain things they didn't understand, but now that we have science we don't really need that anymore. This doesn't mean that I don't have faith; it's just not in God.

Sometimes I think it would be easier if I did believe in God. In the past, my faith in God and Heaven helped me get through some rough times. When I was young, my brother's best friend passed away. Because I did believe in God at the time, I found comfort in the thought that my brother's friend was going to a better place.

But about a year ago, I went through a particularly rough time in my life, and what made it even worse was that I didn't have God to turn to. Two close friends of mine died within two weeks of each other. I was devastated. They were both so young—just out of high school—and they were gone so quickly, so unexpectedly. Unlike when I was younger, I couldn't find solace in the thought that they were now with God, in a better place. This time I had to accept the fact that they were just gone. They no longer existed.

I was so depressed. The pain in my heart was nearly unbearable.

But instead of turning to God, I turned to my friends, and they proved to me that my faith in people was not misplaced. My friends understood what I was going through and did whatever they could to help. They assured me that my friends were no longer suffering or in pain, and that I would always have them in my memories. My friends lent me a shoulder to cry on. One of my best friends even drove an hour to stay with me the evening after one of the funerals—just so I wouldn't be alone. My friends were so supportive; I don't know what I would have done without them.

Finding God

I think that people are God, really. We have the ability to change people's lives. Through little tiny gestures we can really brighten up someone's day.

One day when I was waiting on line to buy a bus ticket home, there was a man ahead of me trying to buy a ticket as well. He was shabbily dressed, his hair tangled, and his face looked as if it hadn't been washed in days. I saw him count out change on the counter as the clerk sadly shook her head, indicating it simply wasn't enough. To the left of this man was a college-age kid, also purchasing a ticket. Seeing the man at the next counter turning his pockets inside out to find more change, the kid pulled a couple of bills out of his wallet and said, "Hey man, I've got you covered." The man accepted the money with a grateful look on his face. I was really touched by this exchange. It proved that there is goodness in the world. Simple things like this random act of kindness ensure my faith in my fellow man.

It's really important that you can trust people. I don't believe in evil. I think everybody has the potential to be truly good, and I think it's natural for us to want to be. That's why you see community service organizations like Key Club, which I've become extremely involved in. And that's why there are soup shelters and places where people can go and receive help. People want to help others.

People really aren't that different from one another. We all have the same feelings and share the same basic dreams. This sameness is what connects us—spiritually—to one another, and this makes us responsible for one another. Life is too precious to turn your back on it.

Making a Difference

I first joined Key Club, a national service organization, because my brother was heavily involved with it. He joined to help bring an ambulance to our town. Key Club meant a lot to my brother, so I decided to become involved, too.

On the local level, I've been very involved in a slew of projects. I chaired the committee that organized volunteers for America's Walk for Diabetes. I participated in the Key Club's service project, the Healthy Kids Festival, and last year I was our club editor. There are many more projects the club participates in, but I pick a few major projects throughout the year that mean a lot to me to help out with, and then volunteer hours whenever they need people to fill in.

I don't believe in altruism. I don't think there's any such thing, which is kind of funny coming from someone who loves community service. I think the reason people help one another is because we get something back from it. When you go out and you rake up the leaves in the park or paint park benches and look at what you've done, you get the satisfaction of doing something really nice and really good. When people smile at you, it's just such a wonderful feeling you get. So I don't think that people do things solely for other people. I think we do it because it comforts us.

I have not completely abandoned my religion. If you study the words of Hebrew prayers, even though they say God, you can think of God as more of a general thing and the prayers are still really, truly nice. To a former believer, they're just beautiful things to say to somebody. Whenever I say the prayers, I think to myself "let this be" rather than "let God do it for us."

I do go to youth group. I do a lot of stuff at my synagogue, even though it may not be for religious reasons. There's still the cultural aspect of Judaism that I really like. And I like being around people who come from backgrounds similar to mine.

I believe in *chai*, which means "life" in Hebrew, and that means basically the sanctity of life is one of the most important things ever. Lately I've been thinking about priorities. It seems that a lot of my peers don't have their priorities straight. They think it's more important to think about who you are going out with or whether you are going to wear Abercrombie and Fitch or Gap. *Chai* is one of my biggest priorities. Life is short no matter how you look at it. So it's important to live life to our best, live life to our fullest, treat other people well, and be happy. If somebody is suffering, it's important that we try to end their suffering. I don't want to see people in pain.

Life is one of the most wonderful things. And it truly is a blessing. I don't know by whom, but it is a blessing.

amanda groaning:
to say
GOOD-BYE

Raised as a Catholic, it wasn't until Amanda was faced with her father's death that this teen learned the true meaning of faith.

Amanda Groaning, as told to Megan Howard

I never realized how important faith was until the day the doctors told us my father was going to die. I had been raised a strict Catholic. I went to both a Catholic grade school and a Catholic high school, so the church and God were fixtures in my life. But what it meant to have faith and how important it was didn't dawn on me until I was sixteen and faced with the reality that my father wasn't going to be around forever.

In 1996, my father became very ill. He had been ill before, but this time it was more serious. This time he wasn't going to get better. I come from a large family, eight children in all, and I'm the seventh. As a result, my father was much older when I was born, so there was always a subconscious knowledge that he would not be there forever, but I never expected it to happen before I finished growing up.

When we were young our mom had been a stay-at-home mom, then when my dad retired, she went to work and he stayed home. Before he was sick, he was home all the time, waking us up in the morning, making sure we did our homework, playing sports with us and taking us to our games. He wasn't perfect, but he was a great dad, and I loved having him around.

Letting Nature Take Its Course

Dad was first put in the hospital in May 1996 for congestive heart failure. He came home right around my sixteenth birthday, but I could tell he wasn't any better. As the summer continued, his health deteriorated even more. He was then placed back into the hospital at the beginning of August. His heart condition was worse, but my mother said that kidney failure was the real problem this time. All of his systems were just shutting down.

The doctor said that my dad would have to be placed in a nursing home in order to get the daily care he needed. My dad would have to take various and enormous amounts of medicine as well as undergo medical procedures such as dialysis in order to maintain a life that was a shadow of his original.

But we all knew my dad wouldn't go for this. He liked to be outside, taking long walks. He wouldn't want to be cooped up inside with people he didn't know taking care of him. My brother had to talk him into getting dialysis the first time. After it was over, my dad said he couldn't do that again.

So after much consideration, my dad told my mom that he wanted to let nature take its course. He couldn't go on living a life that he couldn't live fully.

Finding Faith

This announcement left us all wrestling with the emotions facing us. My father was dying and in pain as his body was shutting down. I expected his death, but at the same time it was a shock. I kind of knew while growing up that he might not be there my whole life, but now it hit me that he wasn't going to see my graduation or any other important events in my life.

I had to push off my grieving and selfish emotions and pray for God to give him ease. I felt horrible that I was, in essence, praying for my father's death and asking him to be taken from me. But my faith was in God to ease my father's suffering more than my own.

I had been unsure of my faith before, but in my prayers—and in my living and my father's dying—I came to realize that I did have faith, in something much bigger than myself, and that connected me to all the cycles of life. That next day my mother went to be with my dad in the hospital and stayed by his side till his last breath.

My father died at 11:30 A.M. on August 19, 1996. My family called from the hospital to let me know he was gone and that they would be home when they could. It was about ten minutes later that something occurred that I feel was a sign of the power of my faith. My sister called from work and asked me to check her messages on three-way. One of the messages was left at 11:33 A.M. We heard my father voice a sigh of relief. It was a sound that we had heard him make countless times. My sister asked me to call the hospital to see if he was okay, and that's when I told her he had died minutes before.

As my family started to arrive back home, each one listened to the message. No one believed this could be true—that my father could have left the message. He had been unable to speak since the night before and had been pronounced dead three minutes before the message was left. However, as each person listened to the sound, each knew it was him.

We all felt he was letting us know he was fine and was giving us the comfort we needed. It felt like a validation—that there is something more to believe in than just the here and now. Once you're gone, you're not just *gone*. There is another realm that we can exist in. This was his last gift to us.

Moving On

My father's dying made me a lot less afraid of death. After my father died, I went on a high school retreat. One of the discussions was about dying and Heaven and death. People were saying, "I don't want to die." But I was very strong in my convictions that death isn't something to be afraid of.

My father's death strengthened my faith—in Catholicism, in God, in life itself. For the first time, I felt as if faith was something real. It was the emotional place where I could go to gather the strength I needed to face all that was happening to me and my family. When I prayed—and I prayed a lot—faith helped me believe I could get through this. And that my father was going to be okay.

Growing up, I learned all the lessons about

Catholicism, but they didn't seem to apply to my life. They didn't speak to how I felt about myself or about the things happening around me. Catholicism gave me the rules and the lessons, but I had to make the connection between them and my life.

All religions give you these tools, but you have to develop faith yourself. Otherwise, you're just going through the motions and doing what you think you're supposed to do. I don't think that really helps anybody. I have a lot of friends who don't feel the same way, but it's probably because they haven't really ever thought of their religion as a part of who they are. They've thought of it as what they have to do to please their parents.

I now try to interact with people in a nicer and more meaningful way. I try not to take things, like relationships, for granted. I've tried to look at where people are coming from before I make a judgment about how they react in a situation. If somebody's having a bad day, I'm not going to blame them. At least, I try not to. Of course, I can't be perfect.

My faith is strong—strong enough to transcend life and death. I know that some people cast faith aside because they think it's a way of deluding yourself from the reality of life. But to me, faith is really the essence of life; it is acknowledging the universal connection that we all share, no matter what religion you follow. We all need to have something greater than ourselves to believe in, and that is our connection to each other.

Chapter 13

jonathan jackson:
the LOVE
of God

Even with three Emmys for his role as Lucky on *General Hospital*, Jonathan Jackson knows it's his faith in God that matters above anything else in his life.

Jonathan Jackson, as told to Jon Barrett

The best way to describe my relationship with God is to compare it to a romance. And in this case, I would compare it to a romance where a boy grows up knowing a girl his whole life and then suddenly realizes one day that he's in love with her.

That's exactly how it happened with God and me. Sure, he's always played *a* role in my life. But now he plays *the* role in my life. Until I was about thirteen, there were times when I only thought about God once or twice a week—when I went to church. Then, when I became a teenager, I developed a passion for listening to tapes and reading books with Christian themes, such as *The Screwtape Letters*, by C. S. Lewis. Looking back now, I realize that God was wooing me with those tapes and books. He was pursuing my heart. And once He got ahold of it, He was all I really wanted. Nothing else mattered as much to me.

True Romance

It's really easy for people my age to have an incredibly boring and fake view of who Jesus Christ is. Part of the problem is that so many people don't understand that when they have a relationship with Jesus, they really *are* involved in a romance. You see, Jesus called himself the bridegroom and he called us the brides. When he came to earth he did so with the heart of a warrior to save us. That's why we all love stories like *Braveheart*, *The Last of the Mohicans*, and Robin Hood so much. They tell a story that mirrors Jesus'— one that is engrained inside our hearts.

Keeping in step with the romance analogy, I've learned in just the past two years that the act of worshiping is like entering the private chamber of your relationship with God. Worship doesn't have to mean

going to church—although there is something powerful about being in the same place as two hundred
other people who know what it feels like to be
redeemed. Worship is more about getting over yourself and putting things in their proper perspective.
When I worship, I sometimes listen to CDs—although
there doesn't always have to be music—and I read my
Bible, and I praise God for creating me, redeeming
me, and for literally changing the way I see the world.
Then I just let His love flow through me and fill my
heart with things I can't even begin to describe.

Before God really started working on me in a
huge way, there was so much self-focus in my life. It
was easier for me to be kind of rude to people. Not
because I was trying to be mean, but because I was
just so concerned about myself. But through
my readings, I learned to put my love for Jesus and
others above any thoughts about myself. As Jesus
said, They'll know if you are my disciples because
you'll love one another. I'm very thankful that God
has showed me how to love people in a way that I
never thought I would be able to.

Putting His Love to the Test

Ironically, though, it was my love for another
person that a few years ago put my relationship with

God to one of its biggest tests. I had known this girl my whole life, so when we started dating it was like I was getting to know a part of my heart that had been there a long time. And when we broke up after only six months, I ended up going through what felt like a lifetime of pain. I had to go to God with that pain, and, in the course of healing, I realized that I had, in a way, put this girl above Him. She was on my mind more than He was. My investment, my time, all that stuff, was in her.

God wanted to show me that I can't put a relationship with a human being over my relationship with Him, so he took her out of the picture. It was as if He was saying, "The only place that you're going to have peace is in me." It hurts me now to think about people, and especially people in my generation, who try to make relationships work without God.

In His Eyes

Everything these people are looking for—all the desires of their heart—can be found in His eyes. But as much as I tell people this, they have to realize for themselves that their hearts are not yet filled. And when they do, that is indeed a gift from

God. You never expect the creator of everything to be that interested in you, because it just doesn't seem possible. But, in my case, He's proven it again and again.

Chapter 14

scott weiland:
back from
the BRINK

Stone Temple Pilots lead singer Scott Weiland emerges from a rocky five-year heroin addiction and a five-month prison stint with his spirits high and his music career once again on the rise.

Scott Weiland, as told to Jeremy Helligar

It feels amazing to be alive and to be able to appreciate the little things in life. That sounds sort of clichéd, but it's the truth. Being in jail is wearing on the soul. It's one of those situations that you can either let break you or you can find some source of strength inside of yourself, like a belief in a higher power. I made it through my ordeal because I found a spiritual source of strength. I don't believe that anything I've gone through happened by mistake. My map was laid out for me. I just had to work my way through it. And here I am.

The roots of my substance-abuse problems go way back. There is a big history of drug and alcohol abuse within my family. At a very young age I remember not feeling quite right with myself, and I wasn't sure why. I don't know if it had anything to do with something that happened to me as a young child. My mother, Sharon, who works in real estate, and my father, Richard, divorced when I was two, but other than the usual ripples that that causes in a person's life, I don't think it had a massive effect on me or on my psyche.

As I neared my junior high school years, between the ages of twelve and fourteen, I began experimenting with alcohol and marijuana. They gave me peace of mind, like a chemical vacation, and got me out of that place in my head that I always felt locked into, a place where I didn't feel as comfortable with myself and my surroundings as my peers seemed to appear. By the time I was a high schooler in Huntington Beach, California, I, like a lot of kids my age, was drinking every weekend. I counted the days, the hours, the minutes until Friday would come around and I could go out and tie one on. After high school I studied liberal arts at Orange Coast College in Costa Mesa, California. I was drinking every night, but I wasn't suffering any consequences. To me, it was just partying.

In 1986, when I was nineteen, I formed Stone Temple Pilots with some of my friends: bassist Robert DeLeo, drummer Eric Kretz and guitarist Dean DeLeo. Six years later we were signed to Atlantic Records. Our first album, *Core*, came out in 1992, sold seven million copies and produced big hits like "Plush" and "Sex Type Thing." In 1994, while we were on the road with the Butthole Surfers, somebody introduced me to heroin. Immediately I felt a difference. Instead of walking into a room paralyzed with fear that everyone was looking at me and judging me—and feeling completely out of sync and out of balance around people I didn't know—I felt at ease and confident. It actually bred super-ego overconfidence, which compensated for those younger years when I didn't feel very good about myself.

I think that early insecurity led to my pursuit of fame. Any person with a desire to be validated and loved by millions of people doesn't really feel comfortable in his own skin. I definitely fall into that category. I searched for validation through a lot of other ways, latching onto anything—pot, alcohol, women—

trying to fill that void, and all it seemed to do was breed a lot of loneliness.

Fame also played a role in my attraction to heroin, which became quite powerful very quickly. But I had a difficult time with the concept of superstardom, and I probably wasn't prepared for it and all the demands and changes that came with it. So I allowed myself to build a lot of negative feelings about it. I became almost resentful of my success.

Law and Disorder

The first time I got busted for possession was in May 1995. I was in the middle of a long spree of trying to kick heroin, and I kept failing miserably. I'd check myself into detox clinics, but I had a hard time with the withdrawal periods. I would always use alcohol to get through them, and being drunk just made me want heroin more.

I was arrested that first time after heading out to a bad part of Pasadena that has a lot of drug dealing, cheap fleabag hotels, prostitutes, junkies, freaks, runaways, vagrants, everything. I pulled up to a motel in a rented Lexus and was spotted very quickly. I was sent to a long-term treatment facility, but it didn't do much good.

I was arrested again in June 1998 in New York

City shortly before a show in support of my solo album, *12 Bar Blues*. I let down a lot of people—my fans, my backing band, Peter Gabriel, who was going to join me onstage for a few songs, and myself.

The guys in STP also suffered. They didn't know how to deal with the situation and had a lot of anger toward me. While I was out of commission they formed a side project called Talk Show, which released a self-titled album in 1997. The previous year, during the making of 1996's *Tiny Music . . . Songs from the Vatican Gift Shop*, I was a mess. We rented this massive mansion in the Santa Inez Valley, and there were pools, basketball courts and tennis courts, everything to provide a wonderful experience. But I'd be locked inside my bedroom, sitting in the walk-in closet with a harpoon in my arm.

Throughout my affair with heroin, I would achieve brief periods of sobriety, ranging from thirty days to four months. I had four months a few times, but I would slip back into it because I didn't know how to get over that feeling of depression I got when I wasn't using heroin. I believed there was a solution for other people, but I didn't believe that it would work for me because I had tried it and it kept failing.

So on September 3, 1999, I found myself in front of a judge for the second time in less than a year. The previous January, after another arrest, the judge had warned me, "This is your last chance. If you blow this one, I'm guaranteeing you a year in county jail." Well, I blew it in July. After being clean and sober for about a month, I overdosed. I was taken to the emergency room and came close to dying.

Behind Bars

That was the last time I got loaded. I detoxed in the hospital, and I've now been free of alcohol and drugs for more than two years—the longest I've ever been clean. But despite my serious resolution to clean up my act after overdosing, the judge kept his promise and sentenced me to a year in jail.

After being there for a month and a half, I came to the conclusion that no matter how hard I tried to control any form of using or drinking I would always end up in the same situation if I didn't give it all up completely. So I made a commitment to myself, a decision that this was not the way I wanted to live my life, and I was able to find some beauty in life even while being incarcerated.

I was paroled on December 30, 1999, after serving five months of the one-year sentence (I got one month's credit for time served earlier). These days the need to get a fix has been, for the most part, removed. There was only one occasion during the first year where even the remote idea of a chemical break sounded appealing. But I knew that getting loaded was simply not an option. I had to sit with my feelings and find a way to get through them.

I was not worried about having a relapse during the summer of 2000 when Stone Temple Pilots hit the road for a U.S. tour with the Red Hot Chili Peppers. The Chili Peppers are friends of ours and they, like us, have gone through some major personal turmoil due to certain members' addiction to heroin.

I also had a support system: I took this guy on tour with me who used to work at one of the first rehab centers that I went to. He's been clean and sober for seventeen years, and he has life experience in how to deal with things that pop up on a day-to-day basis, especially on the road. He's worked with a lot of other musicians who have gotten clean.

Natural High

Sobriety isn't the only positive in my life these days. I got married in May 2000 to Mary Forsberg, who's a model, and we've had our first child. [Scott split with his first wife, Janina, in 1997, after three years of marriage.] I'm glad that it's happening now because it will give me the opportunity to be a young father. Another one of the greatest gifts in my life is my renewed relationship with the band. *No. 4* went platinum, and the "Sour Girl" video, which features Sarah Michelle Gellar, was an MTV hit. And in June 2001 we released our fifth album *Shangri-La Dee Da*.

Having gone through what I have, I'm finally able to appreciate my success. I just hope that others learn from my experiences. A lot of young people think as I did and buy into the rock myth that heroin and other drugs are part of the secret recipe to artistic expression. Well, I'm here to tell you that couldn't be further from the truth.

I think a lot of successful artists had feelings similar to mine while growing up. When they came across a seemingly cure-all chemical, they latched onto it just as I did. A lot of those people were ultimately destroyed. Look at Jimi Hendrix, Janis Joplin and Jim Morrison. For whatever reason, God wants me here for some purpose. Living is really an amazing experience. I feel pretty lucky.

Teen People ®

If you have enjoyed *Faith* then we're sure you'll like receiving *Teen People* magazine every month!

· Go on tour with your favorite bands!

· Visit the sets of top TV shows!

· Meet real-life teens doing really cool things!

· See candid shots of the top celebs at work and play!

· Get the real scoop on dating, school, drugs, love and more!

· Keep up-to-date with the must-have CDs!

If you'd like a *FREE PREVIEW ISSUE* please call 800-284-0200 or go to our website at www.teenpeople.com

TEENS....TEACHERS....PARENTS

Celebrate teens and their achievements!
Do you know a teenager who has made a difference?

Teens today are affecting the world more than at any other time in history. *Teen People®* magazine and HarperCollins Publishers want to celebrate teens making a positive difference in their communities and in our world. Introducing the

TEEN PEOPLE COMMUNITY ACTION AWARDS

Any teen age 13 to 21 who has made a significant contribution to the community is eligible. No act of kindness is too small, no plan too grand. It could take place at school, home or the local hangout. It can be an act of courage or kindness. If a teen you know has touched one heart, or one hundred hearts, we want to know about it.

What to do: In 500 words or less, tell us about the teen who inspires you. Tell us about your community and how this amazing teenager has made it a better place to live. Send your essay, along with the family contact information of the teen to *TEEN PEOPLE* **COMMUNITY ACTION AWARD, HarperCollins Children's Books, 1350 Avenue of the Americas, New York, NY 10019.**

The Award: The teen whose story is the most inspiring and impressive to our distinguished panel of judges will win a $2,500 scholarship, a trip to the star-studded *TEEN PEOPLE* **COMMUNITY ACTION AWARD** Ceremony in New York or Los Angeles in September 2002, a 2-year subscription to *Teen People* magazine, and a selection of books from HarperCollins Publishers. In addition, the winner's name will be announced in an issue of *Teen People*.

Three 1st Prize winners will each receive a $500 scholarship, a trip to the awards ceremony in September 2002, a 1-year subscription to *Teen People* magazine, and a selection of books from HarperCollins Publishers.